IMAGES
of Sport

SWINDON TOWN
FOOTBALL CLUB

IMAGES
of Sport

SWINDON TOWN FOOTBALL CLUB

Compiled by
Richard Mattick

TEMPUS

Tempus Publishing Limited
The Mill, Brimscombe Port,
Stroud, Gloucestershire, GL5 2QG

ISBN 0 7524 2093 3

Typesetting and origination by
Tempus Publishing Limited
Printed in Great Britain by
Midway Clark Printing, Wiltshire

Also available from Tempus Publishing

Birmingham City FC	Tony Matthews	0 7524 1862 9
Crewe Alexandra FC	Harold Finch	0 7524 1545 X
Crystal Palace FC	Nigel Sands	0 7524 1544 1
Forever England	Mark Shaoul/Tony Williamson	0 7524 2042 9
Leeds United FC	David Saffer	0 7524 1642 1
Manchester City FC	David Saffer	0 7524 2085 2
Leicestershire CCC	Dennis Lambert	0 7524 1864 5
Worcestershire CCC	Les Hatton	0 7524 1834 3
Final Tie	Norman Shiel	0 7524 1669 3
The Five Nations Story	David Hands	0 7524 1851 3
The Football Programme	John Litster	0 7524 1855 6
Speedway in East Anglia	Norman Jacobs	0 7524 1882 3
St Andrews Golfing Legends	Stuart Marshall	0 7524 1812 2
Voices of 1966	Norman Shiel	0 7524 2045 3

This is just a small selection of our sports titles. For a full catalogue please contact the Sales Department at the address given above. Alternatively you can telephone on 01453 883300 or e-mail sales@tempus-publishing.com.

Contents

Foreword

I am very pleased to be asked to write a foreword for this superb book depicting the pictorial history of Swindon Town.

Having arrived in Swindon as a fifteen year old in 1961, I could not have imagined all the changes that would occur in the next forty years. Having played my first game in the 1962/63 promotion season, against Notts County (we won 3-1), at the age of seventeen, it is very interesting for me to see pictures of the stadium then and now. During the following ten years, the club had many highs and lows, with another promotion in 1968/69 and a wonderful cup run in the same year – culminating in a memorable Wembley final.

Then the stadium underwent a major transformation with the building of the North Stand, which completely changed the look of the County Ground. Over the following period, supporters have certainly had plaenty of emotional years. There have beentwo play-off finals at Wembley (with two victories), promotion to the Premier League and then relegation from the Premier League in successive seasons – but I am sure that everybody enjoyed the experience. Then change came to the County Ground again, with the new Intel Stand and a wonderful new surface – so different from the mud of my day – provided for the the players.

For my first few years at the club, I soon learned how thrifty our trainer, Harry Cousins, could be and why people spent a lot of time in the treatment room (two lamps and a wooden table). First of all, if you had a hole in your training shoe Harry only gave you one new shoe and not a pair. Secondly, the stories that Harry, and later Kevin Morris told were of Harry's playing days and how he stopped them playing. 'They can't play without their legs' he would say in his Northern accent.

This book has brought back many memories for me and I am sure it will for everybody else who reads it. So a big thankyou to Dick for helping us to relive the past one more time.

Don Rogers

Acknowledgements

I must begin by say that without the help of Wiltshire Newspapers and their staff, in particular photographer Dave Evans, this book would not have been possible. I am also grateful to the board of directors of Swindon Town FC for allowing me access to the trophy cabinet. I would also like to thank Julia Green for letting the club have her father's collection of football mementoes, which I have been able to draw on. Paul Plowman's statistical records, from his Footprints publications (now sadly out of print) have been an invaluable source of reference. I would also like to thank Julie Burbidge for helping with proof-reading. Her non-football specialist eye identified a number of areas of omission which might have made things unintelligible to the general reader. Last, but by no means least, my thanks go to Don Rogers for contributing the introduction, which makes me feel this book has been very worthwhile. Any errors remaining are my own.

Introduction

In recent years there has been some debate as to when Swindon Town FC was actually formed. The club itself celebrated its Centenary in 1981 with a match against Ipswich Town and the amalgamation of St. Marks football team with a club called the Spartans from the Old Town area is usually seen as the event which gave birth to the club. The next key date was probably 1894, when the club began to engage professionals and also became one of the founder members of the Southern League Division One. Town's best performance in these early years came in 1900, when it reached fourth position, but two seasons later it finished bottom of the league. As on so many later occasions, finances dictated the sale of players and but for the work of stalwarts like Sam Allen, the club might well have not survived.

Survive it did, and between 1910 and the outbreak of World War One it enjoyed one of its most successful periods, twice winning the Southern League Championship and twice reaching the semi-final of the FA Cup. The war caused the break-up of this successful team, but in 1920 the creation of Division Three (South) saw Swindon move into the Football League. Their first League victory, over Luton Town, has still not been improved on and forty years were to go by before Swindon had a promotion to celebrate. Indeed, had it not been for the old pals act, Swindon might have lost their League status altogether, for in 1933, 1956 and 1957, they had to aply for re-election. Swindon's cause was not helped by the fact that World War Two saw the club in mothballs, with the ground requisitioned by the War Office and used as a POW camp. Gradually the club got back on its feet, but times were hard and finances were very tight.

It was October 1956 when the arrival of Bert Head transformed the club's prospects. The 1957/58 season saw a remarkable change as, after two consecutive re-elections, Town finished in the top half of the Division Three (South) table and thus earned membership of the nationwide Third Division. Then Bert Head began to develop the youth policy, which soon saw a remarkable group of young players emerge, whose talent helped secure Swindon their first ever promotion in 1963 – when they were runners-up in Division Three and promoted, along with champions Northampton. Despite an initial surge to the top of the Division Two table, two years later Swindon were relegated and several of the talented youngsters moved on to higher division clubs. Bert's Babies, as they were known, had given the supporters a taste of higher quality football while their sale brought much-needed finance to help the new manager, Danny Williams. The canny Yorkshireman made some judicious purchases to play alongside the remaining youngsters, such as Roger Smart, Don Rogers and John Trollope, and in 1969, Town were able to celebrate promotion to Division Two again. It was to be a year of double celebration for, on 15 March, a League Cup final victory over Arsenal gave the club what is arguably its greatest day to date.

When Danny Williams moved on to Sheffield Wednesday, new manager Fred Ford captured some international trophies, but again the prize of Division One football eluded Swindon. The 1970s and early '80s saw something of a slump in the club's fortunes and although Bobby Smith took the club to another League Cup semi-final, by 1984 they were languishing in Division Four. It was from this low ebb that Lou Macari was to build the greatest period of success in the club;'s history. A Fourth Division championship in 1986 was to be followed by a promotion, through the play-offs, to Division Two. Lou was to take Town close to another promotion play-off, but they lost out to Crystal Palace and Lou departed to West Ham in 1989. The chairman, Brian Hillier, was astute enough to recruit Ossie Ardiles as as a replacement.

It was to be Ossie who would lead Swindon to a 1-0 play-off triumph over Sunderland and the achievement of top-flight football. However, Swindon's position in Division One was to last for only ten days before a Football League tribunal relegated Swindon by two divisions for illegal payments. This was subsequently reduced to one division on appeal to the Football Association. Ossie then left to take over as manager of Newcastle United, but Swindon were fortunate in being able to appoint Glenn Hoddle as his replacement. Glenn's skills, both as a player on the pitch and as manager off it, saw Swindon reach Wembley in 1993 for another play-off final. It proved to be one of the most thrilling play-offs of all, with Swindon squandering a three-goal lead over Leicester City before a Paul Bodin penalty clinched Premiership status for Swindon.

Glenn departed to Chelsea and his number two, John Gorman, took over. The stay in the Premiership was to last only a season but was to leave fans with a lifetime of memories and much respect for the quality of football that Swindon had played during that 1993/94 season. Swindon slipped to mid-table in Division One, and after defeat at Bristol City, John Gorman was sacked and replced with Steve McMahon. He was unable to stop Swindon sliding to Division Two, which he said left him feeling 'Lower than a snake's belly' but led Swindon back the following season to become Division Two champions. By this time, the gap between the football haves and have-nots was increasing. Higher prices were being charged to try and pay higher wages and to buy some success, but this did not work out and simply led to a spiral of falling gates. McMahon departed and was replaced by Jimmy Quinn, who proved a popular choice as manager. By now, however, Swindon were losing money at an alarming rate and Quinn was forced to sell quality players such as Nhda and Hay and allow others, like Walters, to leave. The club foundered into administration, was relegated and Quinn was sacked. Hopefully, the club will survive and there is talk of a bright tomorrow – but in times of trouble it is no bad thing to have a pictorial reminder of the club's proud past.

One

Early Days

Perhaps the earliest photograph ever taken of a Swindon Town team. Although the club marked its own centenary in 1881, more recent research suggests that Swindon were actually in existence in 1879. No list of players' names was attached to the photograph but among those playing for the club at the time were the Revd William Pitt (club founder), R.H. Barnett (captain), W. Woolford, A. Watson, G. Rawlings, C. Humphreys, T. Hancock, W. Cockbill, ? Davies and J. Cook.

A team photograph from the 1891/92 season.

An artist's impression of Jimmy Munro, usually thought to be the first professional player employed by Swindon Town. He contracted pneumonia following a match with Tottenham and died shortly afterwards.

J. MUNRO

In Loving & Affectionate Memory

OF

JAMES MUNRO,

Captain of the Swindon Town Football Club,

Who departed this Life, Jan. 4, 1899,

AGED 28 YEARS.

A star from out our ranks has gone;
A light which shone the best :
No more he'll play the manly game,
For Jimmy has gone to rest.

-:o:-

Gone from us, but not forgotten,
Never shall thy memory fade ;
Sweetest thoughts shall ever linger
Round the spot where thou art laid.

The front and reverse of an *In memoriam* card published following Jimmy's untimely demise.

11

Swindon, under this agreement, built their first stand in 1896 with the help of a £300 loan from local brewers, Arkells.

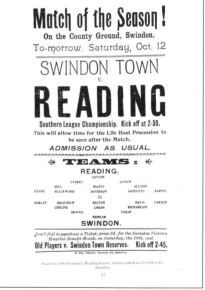

Left: Bob Menham, a former Grenadier Guardsman who had played for Everton in the 1897 Cup Final, joined Swindon in 1898. He kept goal for the club up until 1903 and later joined the board of directors. *Right:* A poster for a match at the County Ground against local rivals Reading in 1901. The game resulted in a 4-0 win for Reading.

This picture was taken in August 1902. The players are listed in team order on the reverse: R.W. Menham, J.O. Brian, A. Jones, H. Oakden, C. Bannister, J.B. Cowley, T. Davis, J. Poppitt, M. Neyland, J. Pugh, W. Kirby.

Personalities of the Players.

R. W. MENHAM *(Goal)*, **6ft. 1in.**; **Weight, 13 stone.**
Now in his fifth Season with the Swindon Town F.C. "Bob" has seen great service, notably with Everton, with which Club he played in the celebrated English Cup Final against Aston Villa (supposed to be the best Final on record).

J. O'BRIEN *(Right Back)*, **5ft. 7in.**; **Weight, 12 stone.**
First came from Scotland to play for Clitheroe, a Lancashire League Team; from there to Reading, Blackburn Rovers, and last Season Aberdeen. He came South again, doubtless with the intention to maintain the fine reputation he gained when with Reading.

W. HOLMES (20) *(Left Back)*, **5ft. 9½in.**; **Weight, 12 stone.**
One of the youngsters of the Team. He is a Preston born lad, and has been with North End Reserves two Seasons.

H. OAKDEN (25) *(Right Half-Back)*, **5ft. 8½in.**; **Weight, 11st. 10.**
Like his predecessor (Georgie Richardson), was an Outside Right, but since playing Half-Back last Season at Portsmouth has not been shifted. He finished in remarkably good style last April.

C. BANNISTER (26) *(Centre Half)*, **5ft. 8½in.**; **Weight, 11 stone.**
Started playing with Everton Combination as an Amateur, then as a Professional to Manchester City where he remained two Seasons; from there he was transferred to Lincoln City and finished his fifth Season with them.

J. B. COWLEY (24) *(Left Half-Back)*, **5ft. 8in.**; **Weight, 11st. 7.**
Was two Seasons with Hinckley Town (a Midland League Team), then was signed by Lincoln City where he remained three Seasons.

T. DAVIS (20) *(Outside Right)*, **5ft. 6in.**; **Weight, 10 stone 7.**
Now in his third Season with the First Team.

J. POPPITT (23) *(Inside Right)*, **5ft. 9½in.**; **Weight, 11 stone 7.**
Played for Wellington Town in the Birmingham League; was signed on by Wolverhampton Wanderers, where he stayed two Seasons.

M. NEYLAND (24) *(Centre or Inside Left)*, **5ft. 7½in.**; **Weight, 11st.**
Came South to Chatham, from which Club, when defunct, he went to New Brompton, and from there to Bolton Wanderers.

J. PUGH (26) *(Inside Left or Centre)*, **5ft. 7½in.**; **Weight, 11 stone.**
Played for Rock Ferry, from there to Gravesend, and last season Wellingboro'.

A. EDWARDS (26) *(Outside Left)*, **5ft. 7in.**; **Weight, 11 stone.**
Played for Swindon more or less for six Seasons.

W. HUNTER *(Trainer).*
5 years with Darwen, 3 years with Bury. Both these teams won their way from from the Second Division to the First whilst under his care.

Photographs and brief details of players for the 1902/03 season. Published by William T. Anderson, one of the club's directors, it sold for 2d, with proceeds going to club funds.

THE SWINDON TOWN FOOTBALL CO., LTD.

(Incorporated under the Companies' Acts, 1862 to 1890.)

SHARE CAPITAL £1500, IN 3000 ORDINARY SHARES OF 10/- EACH.

No. *769*

ORDINARY SHARE CERTIFICATE.

This is to certify that *W. F. Cowley* of *94 Goddard Avenue Swindon* is the holder of *one* Ordinary Shares of Ten Shillings each, No. *1778 & 1779* both inclusive, of the Swindon Town Football Company, Limited, subject to the Memorandum and Articles of Association of the said Company.

Given under the Common Seal of the said Company the *11th* day of *February* 19*29*.

Eddie Thomas
A. E. Bullock } Directors.

Samuel Allen Secretary.

R. ASTILL & SONS, PRINTERS, SWINDON.

Swindon Town became a limited company in 1897 and this is an example of an early share certificate.

The 1904/05 squad, which finished only two places from the foot of the Southern League, pose in front of the Swindon Cricket Club pavilion. From left to right, back row: Milligan, Dixon, Hemmings, Alterbury, Archer. Third row: Sam Allen (secretary), Woolf, Oakden, Stringfellow (captain), Cowley, Jones, Tom Wiltshire (trainer). Second row: Kirby, Poppitt, Lean, Bradworth, Chalmers. Front row: Toombs, Sanderson, Pugh.

A typical wage bill from 1903.

W.E. Dec 19 1903

Hemming   1 0 0
Milligan 10/- ded 1 10 0
Atterbury 5/-   1 15 0
Wolfe   2 0 0
Bannister   2 0 0
Logan   2 0 0
Oakden 5/-   1 0 0
Cowley   2 5 0
Green   2 10 0
Bendoworth   2 0 0
Hogan 5/-   1 10 0
Pugh   2 0 0
Peer   1 15 0
Wiltshire   1 15 0
Ludlow   - 4 0
Archer   - 5 0
McKardock   - 5 0
                 _____
Total £ 35. 14 .0.

P. CHAMBERS

Peter Chambers joined Swindon from Bristol City in 1907. He was captain of the team for two years but, when Billy Silto joined Town from Middlesbrough, he lost his place in the team. He retired in 1912 having made 90 Southern League appearances for Town.

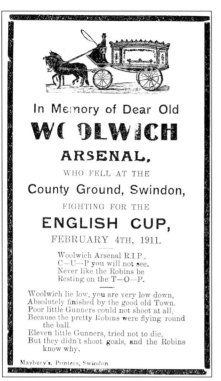

In Memory of Dear Old
WOOLWICH
ARSENAL,
WHO FELL AT THE
County Ground, Swindon,
FIGHTING FOR THE
ENGLISH CUP,
FEBRUARY 4TH, 1911.

Woolwich Arsenal R.I.P.,
C–U–P you will not see.
Never like the Robins be
Resting on the T–O–P.

Woolwich lie low, you are very low down,
Absolutely finished by the good old Town.
Poor little Gunners could not shoot at all,
Because the pretty Robins were flying round
the ball.
Eleven little Gunners, tried not to die,
But they didn't shoot goals, and the Robins
know why.

Maybury's, Printers, Swindon

In Memory of
Notts
County,
WHO FELL FIGHTING FOR THE
ENGLISH CUP,
(Second Round)
At the County Ground, Swindon
FEBRUARY 3rd, 1912.

The "County of Notts" went down
In the gale of the Second Round.
The good ship is now no more,
And the noble crew are drowned ;
But the "Robins Red" for Palace bound
Is gay as a boat can be,
When home is reached and the Cup is won,
May we all be there to see.

Swindon 2   **Notts** 0.

Spoof *In memoriam* cards like these were common at this time. Swindon's goal in the match with Arsenal was scored by Bob Jefferson and Town went on to reach the fourth round of the FA Cup in 1911, losing 3-1 to Chelsea. The defeat of Notts County was part of Swindon's run to the semi-final in 1912. Bob Jefferson and Freddie Wheatcroft were the Town scorers in the 2-0 win.

This card was printed to commemorate Swindon Town winning the Southern League in 1911.

Swindon reached the semi-final of the FA Cup in both 1910 and 1912. They lost 2-0 to Newcastle in 1910 and 1-0 in a replay in 1912 with Barnsley. This photograph includes all the players who played in the two matches.

Swindon won the Dubonnet Cup, which was contested in Paris on 5 May 1910, by defeating the other losing FA Cup semi-finalists, Barnsley, 2-1. This picture, taken in 1966, showed the three surviving members of that team: Jock Walker, Bob Jefferson and Tommy Bolland.

MILTON
SWINDON.F.C

HAMPTON JUST BIFFED INTO BROWNLIE, AND THE GAME WAS WON.

SIMPSON SOMETIMES SEEMED TO FADE AWAY WHEN HE GOT NEAR JOHN WALKER.

FRAE BLANTYRE

THE NORTHERN SKIPPER WAS A VERY HARD-HEADED SCOT.

THE OLD FIRM PENNINGTON AND CROMPTON

FLEMING HAD A LOT UP HIS SLEEVES. PERHAPS THAT WAS WHY MEN KEPT THEM DOWN.

LEO

ENGLAND V. SCOTLAND.

Swindon v Swindon; Fleming and Walker on opposite sides in the England
v Scotland match, played on Saturday 5 April 1913.

Top left: 'A light-haired son of Beith who Southward came a faring' is how a poem in *Athletic News* described Jock Walker, a Scottish international, who played at right-back in Swindon's two semi-final teams. He later ran a fish and chip shop in Manchester Road. *Above:* A. Milton joined Swindon from Sunderland. He made 27 Southern League appearances in Swindon's team during 1914/15 season. He volunteered for the Army and was killed in action in 1915. *Left:* Two Swindon players, Fleming and Walker, featured in this cartoon of the England *v.* Scotland match of 1913.

Two

Between the Wars

This picture of a section of the crowd gives an idea of what the atmosphere must have been like. The proximity of the spectators to the touchline must have been a hair-raising experience for both wingers and full-backs alike.

SWINDON TOWN FOOTBALL COMPANY LIMITED.

STATEMENT OF ACCOUNTS, SEASON 1917-18

Dr.	£	s.	d.	Cr.		£	s.	d.
To Balance brought forward	99	9	8	By Travelling Expenses, Amounts Paid to other Clubs, Gate Expenses, Rates, Taxes, Insurance, Salaries &c.	....	316	14	5
Gates, Amounts received from other Clubs, &c., &c., ...	276	8	3	Entertainment Tax (Paid)		58	19	11
,, Entertainment Tax (Collected)	59	0	11	Charities.—Military 12 17 6				
,, Gates, Charity Matches	37	17	6	Victoria Hospital 4 5 10				
				Wilts Nursing Home 4 5 10				
				Prisioners of War Fund 16 8 4				
						37	17	6
				Balance in hand	....	59	4	6
Total	£472	16	4	Total		£472	16	4

Statement of Liabilities and Assets, April 30th, 1918

LIABILITIES	£	s.	d.	£	s.	d.	ASSETS.			£	s.	d.
Share Capital							Balance in Bank			58	17	5
3000 at 10/-							Balance in Secretary's Hands			7	1	
Subscribed Capital										59	4	6
1573 at 10/-	786	10	0				Deposit South Eastern League			5	0	0
Less unpaid	107	0	0				Club Properties					
				679	10	0	April 30th 1917	902	10 0			
Sundry Creditors	....		....	30	0	0	less 5% depreciation	45	2 6			
Rent	....	....	....	60	0	0				857	7	6
				769	10	0						
Balance in favour of Club			....	152	2	0						
				£921	12	0				£921	12	0

Messrs. H. CHEGWIDDEN, T. KIMBER, T. PHIPPS, G. R. PLAISTER, and H. W. THOMAS, retire by rotation, and being eligible, offer themselves for re-election. Nominations for the Directorate must be in the Secretary's hands three days previous to the Annual General Meeting.

We hereby certify that our requirements as Auditors have been complied with, and that in our opinion the Balance Sheet is properly drawn up, so as to exhibit a true and correct view of the state of the Company's affairs as shewn by the Books of the Company.

May 10th, 1918.

H. W. THOMAS, *Treasurer.*
S. ALLEN, *Secretary*

A. C. BOOTH, } *Auditors.*
S. J. THOMAS, }

The change in monetary value is shown by the balance sheet for the 1917/18 season.

Town players for the first League campaign. Their 9-1 victory at home in the first match with Luton is still the biggest League win in the club's history.

SWINDON TOWN'S PLAYERS.

F. Hawley was a centre half who clocked up 90 appearances for Swindon during their first three seasons in the Football League.

Harold Fleming won 9 caps for England. This statue of him by Carl Atwood stands in the foyer of the club to this day.

THE FLEMING TESTIMONIAL.

A presentation to Harold Fleming (third left) following his retirement from football. Harold ran a sports shop in Commercial Road, until his death in 1955.

Left: F. Thomson, who was signed from Manchester City, made only 7 League appearances for Swindon, all in the 1927/28 season. This photograph, from a postcard issued by Prothero & Simmons, would seem to indicate that images of all players were made available for supporters to purchase – although the numbers that have survived are small. *Right:* J. Bourne joined Swindon from Bolton Wanderers in 1926 and made 41 League appearances in goal for Swindon. He later worked as a local barber in Victoria Road.

The 1926/27 season saw Swindon score over 100 League goals and Harry Morris set an individual scoring record of 47. However, too many goals conceded and a broken leg sustained by Alec Wall meant any hopes of promotion were not realised by this squad.

Burton's the tailors sponsored this fixture list for the 1927/28 season.

Goalkeeper Ted Nash and centre half Viggars defend the Swindon goal in an FA Cup fourth round replay in 1929, which saw Swindon defeat Burnley 3-2.

Bertie Denyer, the Swindon Town winger, featured in a John Player & Sons card series of footballers in 1928.

Town were drawn to play the mighty Arsenal in the FA Cup fifth round in 1929. Here, Wally Dickenson (left), the Town skipper, shakes hands with Tom Parker, the Arsenal skipper, before a goalless draw at the County Ground.

SWINDON TOWN FOOTBALL COMPANY, Limited.

Incorporated under the Companies Acts 1862 to 1907.

CAPITAL - £1,500

Divided into 3,000 Shares of 10/- each.

Thirty-Fourth Annual Report and Balance Sheet

MAY 2nd, 1931.

President.—FRED COLLARD, Esq.

Vice-President.—H. W. THOMAS, Esq.

Directors—

Mr. H. CHEGWIDDEN (Chairman).

Mr. A. E. BULLOCK	Mr. E. HILL	Mr. H. PROSSER
,, H. COULING	,, T. C. NEWMAN	,, J. TILBURY
,, S. GRAY	,, C. R. PALMER	,, J. WHITE

Bankers—

LLOYDS BANK, LTD., BRIDGE STREET, SWINDON.

Auditors—

Messrs. A. C. BOOTH & S. J. THOMAS.

Hon. Treasurer—

C. R. PALMER, Esq.

Secretary and Registered Offices.—

SAMUEL ALLEN, 44, KENT ROAD, SWINDON.

DIRECTORS' REPORT.

In presenting the thirty fourth Statement of Accounts, the Directors regret that for the first time in 24 years they have to declare a deficit amounting to £342 : 0 : 10. The loss on the Season's working amounting to £1984 : 4 : 2. If the £828 received from Donations, £79 from New Shares, is added to this it will be seen how disastrous the past season has been.

It will be seen that the receipts of Div. III. and also those of the Reserve Team have again decreased The average working out, Div. III 4,910, Cash £276, Southern League 1,233, Cash £28 London Combination 1,520, Cash £40, these decreases and the early exit from the English Cup contributed in great measure to the great loss.

The Directors are unanimous of opinion that drastic economy must be exercised, and the only means at their disposal is to reduce the wage bill considerably by engaging a less number of professionals, and by retiring from the Southern League and London Combination, thus saving heavy travelling expenses. Resignation to these competitions have been sent, and application has been made for admission to the Western League, Div. II.

The Practice Match realised £198 : 16 : 6, of which £167 : 6 : 6 was handed to the Victoria Hospital, thus making the sum of nearly £1,500 in ten years to that deserving institution.

Mr. H. Chegwidden, who had been acting Chairman during the long lamentable illness of the late Mr. A. J. L. White was appointed Chairman for the current season.

Apart from the sum of £118 contributed by the President and Directors, the sum of £710 : 14 . 10 has been contributed by the Special Directors Appeal, Ground Stewards, Wilts and Somerset Police Match, Old Pro's. Match, and the Supporters' Club. These sums are without parallel in so short a time, and in a town of this population. The Directors cannot sufficiently express their deep appreciation of these efforts, and desire to tender thanks to all who contributed and worked.

The Directors desire once again to place on record their appreciation of the services of Dr. Gordon Young, Hon. Doctor, The Ground Stewards, The Auditors, Messrs. Booth and S. J. Thomas, the Amateur Members of the team, and also the members of St. John's Ambulance Brigade.

Five of the Directors, viz., Messrs. A. E. Bullock, T. C. Newman, C. R. Palmer, H. Prosser and J. Tilbury retire by rotation, but being eligible, offer themselves for re-election.

Nominations for the Directorate must be in the Secretary's hands three days previous to the Annual

The impact of the Depression on football is seen in this 1931 directors' report on a balance sheet, which shows the first deficit in twenty-four years.

T. W. PHILLIPSON

D. H. MORRIS

Two players of the inter-war period as they were portrayed in a club handbook, in which they both wrote articles. Tom Phillipson scored 24 goals in 87 appearances between 1921 and 1923. His exploits were surpassed by Harry Morris, who was to be the club's all-time leading scorer with 215 goals in 260 appearances.

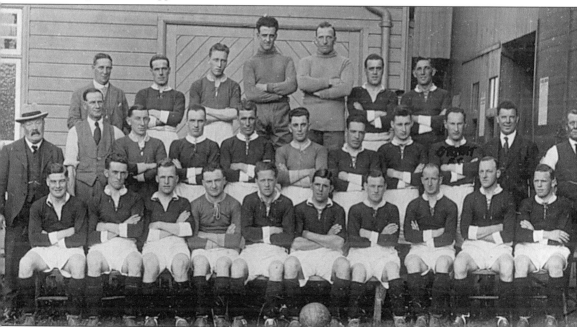

The Town squad that reached the fifth round. They finally went out at Highbury in a 1-0 defeat, having been exempt from the early stages and beaten Newcastle in the third round.

DO YOU REMEMBER ?

A. E. DENYER
1914-30

D. C. BEW
1923-30

A. ARCHER
1921-31

W. DICKENSON
1924-30

J. EDDLESTON
1926-32

A. WALL
1925-28

Six inter-war heroes. Bertie Denyer starred in a 2-0 defeat of Manchester United at Old Trafford in 1930; Danny Bew kept the great Hughie Gallacher quiet when Town beat Newcastle 2-0 in 1929 (a match in which schoolboy international Bob Archer also played); Wally Dickenson scored 20 goals for Swindon, with all but one of them coming from the penalty spot; Joe Eddleston scored 64 goals for Swindon before joining Accrington Stanley in 1932; Alec Wall suffered a broken leg on Christmas Day 1925 playing against Merthyr Town – he was Swindon's playmaker and but for this injury Town might have gone on to promotion.

An Agreement

made the _15th_ day of _June_ 19_34_ between _S. Allen_ of _Swindon_ in the COUNTY OF _Wilts_ the Secretary of and acting pursuant to Resolution and Authority for and on behalf of the _SWINDON TOWN_ FOOTBALL CLUB, of _Swindon_ (hereinafter referred to as the Club) of the one part and _Cecil John Green_ of _12 Armstrong St Swindon_ in the County of _Wilts_ Professional Football Player (hereinafter referred to as the Player) of the other part **Whereby** it is agreed as follows :—

1. The Player hereby agrees to play in an efficient manner and to the best of his ability for the Club.

2. The Player shall attend the Club's ground or any other place decided upon by the Club for the purposes of or in connection with his training as a Player pursuant to the instructions of the Secretary, Manager, or Trainer of the Club, or of such other person, or persons, as the Club may appoint. [This provision shall not apply if the Player is engaged by the Club at a weekly wage of less than One Pound, or at a wage per match.]

3. The Player shall do everything necessary to get and keep himself in the best possible condition so as to render the most efficient service to the Club, and will carry out all the training and other instructions of the Club through its representative officials.

4. The Player shall observe and be subject to all the Rules, Regulations, and Bye-laws of The Football Association. and any other Association, League, or Combination of which the Club shall be a member. And this Agreement shall be subject to any action which shall be taken by The Football Association under their Rules for the suspension or termination of the Football Season, and if any such suspension or termination shall be decided upon, the payment of wages shall likewise be suspended or terminated, as the case may be.

5. The Player shall not engage in any business or live in any place which the Directors (or Committee) of the Club may deem unsuitable.

Cecil Green, who played for the reserves, never made it to the first team, although in later life he was both chairman and president of the club. His contract for 1934 gives an idea of the restrictions placed on players at the time.

DEATH OF 'DADDY' BALL.

Former Swindon Town
F.C.'s Groundsman.

A FOOTBALL ENTHUSIAST.

"Daddy" Ball, champion ticket seller of Swindon, and one of the best supporters the Town Football Club ever had, died at his home, 154, Drove-road, Swindon, early yesterday. He would have been 88 on the last day of this month.

Though stone deaf, Mr. Alfred Ball always had a cheery smile for every-one. Groundsman at the County Ground for more than 20 years, he had his heart and soul in the game of football, and long after he retired, on reaching the age of 80, would wander

Left: The Football League marked its Jubilee in 1938 by presenting all clubs with a beautiful memorial print. Swindon's still hangs just outside the boardroom door at the County Ground. *Right:* A popular County Ground character was 'Daddy' Ball, who probably spent more time on the pitch than the players. His death was marked by this article in the *Evening Advertiser*.

The squad for the 1937/38 season, which reached the FA Cup fourth round, defeating First Division Grimsby Town along the way. The officials in the picture are manager Ted Vizard (far left, middle row), club secretary Sam Allen (far right, middle row) and trainer Frank Martin (far right, behind Allen).

Iron man Harry Cousins joined Swindon in 1932. A pillar of strength in the 1930s, he once played an entire season with a broken bone in his foot. He made only a few appearances after the Second World War, retiring in 1947 to become the club trainer.

Frank Wildman did not have the best of luck with injuries, but here he can be seen advancing from goal in a match with Watford. The other Town player in the centre foreground is Ted Batchelor. Town won this match, which was played on 24 September 1938, by 3 goals to nil. Ben Morton scored twice, the other goal coming from a Cliff Francis penalty. Swindon finished the 1938/39 season, the last to be completed before the Second World War, in ninth position.

1939 - 1945
SERGT. ALAN FOWLER
4TH DORSETS
L.A.C. JAMES IMRIE
R.A.F.
SERGT. JAMES OLNEY
COLDSTREAM GUARDS.

Alan 'Foxie' Fowler, James Imrie and James Olney all played for the Town in the inter-war period and died in action during the Second World War. They are commemorated by this plaque in the main entrance to the County Ground.

Three
In the Doldrums

League football returned to the County Ground in 1946. The squad in this picture took Swindon to a creditable fourth position with Bill Stephens' 26 League goals heading the scoring chart. From left to right, back row: Mills, Woodman, Saunders, Burton, Boulton, Sturgess, Onslow, Trim, Young. Middle row: Martin (trainer), Cousins, Ithell, Parkhouse, Bingham, Lloyd, Lovesey, Emery, Painter, Davis (reserve team trainer). Front row: Page (secretary-manager), Stephens, Denyer, Jones, Stephens, W. Lucas, H. Lucas, Derrick, Edwards, Williams, Blount (assistant secretary).

Swindon Town players and officials for the 1948/49 campaign. From left to right, back row: A. Cowie, G. Hunt, A. White, S. Burton, F. Boulton, A. Young, H. Worrall, W. Lloyd. Middle row: H. Cousins, C. Daniels, J. Corbett, C. Goffey, L. Onslow, J. Ithell, G. Kaye, P. Bingham, R. Timms, R. Peart, E. Painter, A.S. Davies, H. Martin (trainer). Front row: E. Blount (assistant secretary), H. Lunn, R. Onslow, G. Patterson, M. Owen, T. Dawson, M. Jones, P. Jackson, G. Williams, J. Bain, Louis A. Page (secretary-manager).

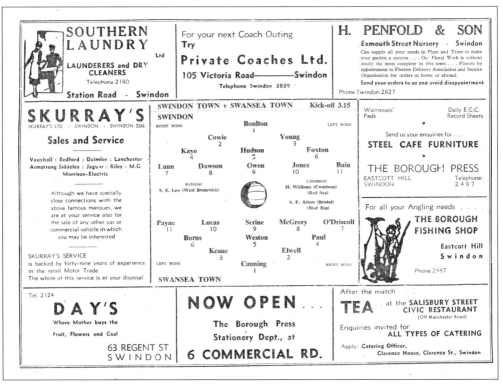

The centre spread of a programme cover for the last home game of the 1948/49 season, in which a goal by Maurice Owen gave Swindon a 1-0 victory.

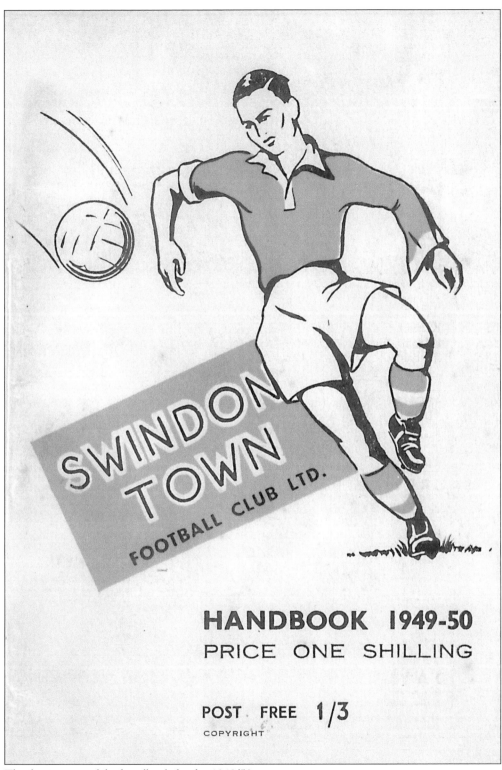

SWINDON TOWN
FOOTBALL CLUB LTD.

HANDBOOK 1949-50
PRICE ONE SHILLING

POST FREE 1/3
COPYRIGHT

The front cover of the handbook for the 1949/50 season.

F. BOULTON   S. BURTON   D. RYLANDS   A. WHITE

A. YOUNG   W. LLOYD   G. HUNT   A. COWIE

G. H. KAYE   J. FOXTON   G. HUDSON   W. J. ITHELL

P. JACKSON   E. PAINTER   R. ONSLOW   H. LUNN

The 1949/50 handbook contained these player portraits.

T. DAWSON   M. OWEN   W. M. JONES   J. BAIN

A. WHEELER   J. SIMNER   C. WHITESIDE   J. THOMAS

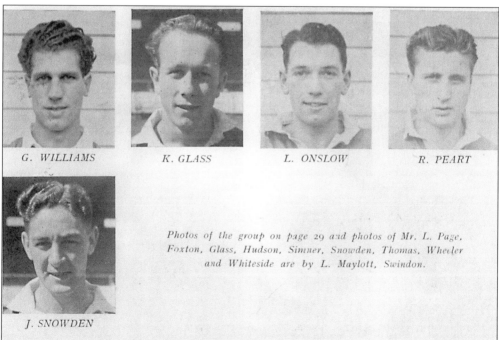

G. WILLIAMS   K. GLASS   L. ONSLOW   R. PEART

Photos of the group on page 29 and photos of Mr. L. Page, Foxton, Glass, Hudson, Simner, Snowden, Thomas, Wheeler and Whiteside are by L. Maylott, Swindon.

J. SNOWDEN

The team ended the season in fourteenth position, with Morris Jones (13) and Owen (10) leading the scoring.

The playing staff for the 1950/51 season line up in front of the old North Stand. The plaque behind goalkeeper Sam Burton's head was a memorial to Swindon Town players killed in the First World War. It seems to have disappeared when the stand was demolished. From left to right, back row: E. Painter, J. Clifford, G. Hunt, D. Ryland, S. Burton, N. Upritchard, G. Paterson, W. Lloyd, L. Lewis. Middle row: C. Daniels, H. Cousins, A. Cowie, E. Batchelor, J. Foxton, L. Onslow, M. Bines, G. Hudson, H. May, G. Jackson, A. Wheeler, G. Williams, H. Martin. Front row: L.A. Page (secretary-manager), W. Millar, J. Court, J. Simner, M. Owen, H. Kaye, R. Peebles, R. Onslow, R. Peart, J. Thomas, J. Bain, A.S. Davies (assistant secretary).

Left: Dickie Blunt, who left the club in 1950, was a schoolmaster who was made a life member of Swindon Town FC and awarded the Football League long service medal for his administrative work. *Right:* Harry Martin, club trainer during this period.

The squad for the 1955/56 season, which was to prove one of the least successful in the club's history. They finished bottom of the Third Division (South), but were successful in applying for re-election. From left to right, back row: J. Fox (captain, inset), G. Hunt, P. Hilton, S. Burton, C. Gill, M. Page, S. Thompson, R. Onslow (inset). Middle row: H. Cousins (trainer), E. Batchelor, B. Farr, R. Jackson, G. Hudson, D. Scarlett, G. Williams, J. Cross, H. Martin (assistant trainer). Front row: A. Micklewright (inset), D. Gibson, R. Edwards, M. Owen, A. McShane, J. Brennan, R. Sampson, E. Edds, R. Johnson (inset).

George Hunt served in the Desert Rats during World War Two. On his return to civilian life, he was spotted playing for Ferndale and was to become a dependable right-back who made over 300 appearances for Town.

Sam Burton, who made 463 appearances for the Town in a career stretching from the 1940s to the '60s.

George Hudson joined Swindon from Portsmouth in 1948. His height of 6 foot 3 inches and weight of fifteen stone led to him being called Garth. He made 401 appearances for Town before his career ended in 1959.

Four

Bert's Babies

Bert Head was assistant manager of Bury when he was appointed manager of Swindon in 1956.

Bill Roost was signed by Bert Head from Bristol Rovers for £2,000. Seen here in cartoon form, Bill fell out with Bert and moved on to play for Stonehouse.

A position of fourth in the table in 1957/58 was enough to earn Town a place in the national Third Division when the Third Division North and South system ended. This was the squad which began to turn the tide of Swindon's fortunes. From left to right, back row: N. Swingler, D. Reeves, G. Hunt, L. Williams, S. Burton, R. Chandler, J. Lee, P. Chamberlain. Middle row: H. Cousins, J. Neal, J. Richards, F. Omahony, G. McDonald, G. Hudson, V. Jack, S. Earl, W. Roost, J. Cross, E. Stuttard. Front row: A. Moore, R. Agar, R. Edwards, A. Darcy, R. Morse (secretary), B. Head (manager), M. Owen, A. Micklewright, J. Fountain, E. Thompson. Insets: L. Clayton, R. Sampson, J. Skull.

Amateur fundraising was very much the order of the day in the 1960s and this picture of the Supporters' Club officials and committee shows how freely people gave of their time to help put thousands of pounds in the club's coffers.

Jack Smith at centre forward and Ken McPherson at centre half added a balance of experience to the youthful enthusiasm of Bert Head's team.

Bill Paul's cartoons were an attractive feature of the *Football Pink* in the late 1950s and early '60s. This one featured the contrasting fortunes of the two 'keepers in Town's FA Cup first round tie with Kettering played on 4 November 1961. The match, on which the cartoon is based, ended in a 2-2 draw at the County Ground and paved the way for a 3-0 victory for Kettering.

Maurice Owen started as a centre forward but ended his career playing at centre half or full-back. He made over 450 appearances for Town and was their leading League scorer, in no fewer than six seasons.

Keith Morgan was born in Trowbridge and progressed through the club's junior teams to become captain of Swindon in succession to Maurice Owen.

Swindon faced the nightmare of all League clubs in 1962, a trip to Yeovil. They overcame the terrors of the dreaded slope winning 2-0, with goals from Ernie Hunt and Cliff Jackson. In this picture, Mike Turner, in cap, is watched by Ken McPherson as he punches clear.

Cliff Jackson, Maurice Owen (number 2) and Keith Morgan are among the players looking on as Mike Turner deals with a high ball in a Cup match at Luton Town's Kenilworth Road ground on 26 January 1963. Cliff Jackson scored both goals in Town's 2-0 win. Their cup run was ended by a 5-1 home defeat by Everton.

RIGHT WING　　　　SWINDON　　　　LEFT WING

Turner

Dawson (2)　　　　Trolope (3)

Morgan (4)　　McPherson (5)　　Woodruff (6)

Summerbee (7)　Hunt (8)　Stevens (9)　Smart (10)　Jackson (11)

Swindon Colours:
RED SHIRTS, WHITE SHORTS

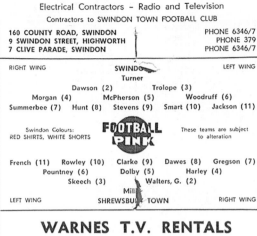

These teams are subject to alteration

French (11)　Rowley (10)　Clarke (9)　Dawes (8)　Gregson (7)

Pountney (6)　　Dolby (5)　　Harley (4)

Skeech (3)　　Walters, G. (2)

Mill

LEFT WING　　SHREWSBURY TOWN　　RIGHT WING

WARNES T.V. RENTALS
TO BE SURE
51 Commercial Road – Swindon – Phone 6486
and Branches

The centre spread of the programme for the match which saw Swindon clinch their first ever League promotion on 4 May, 1963. Apart from the spelling mistake concerning Trollope, the Swindon side, in which only Ken Mcpherson had cost a transfer fee, played as per the programme and Roger Smart scored the only goal.

Part of the expectant crowd for the match with Shrewsbury. These spectators would see Swindon clinch their first ever promotion, when they finished runners-up to Northampton Town in Division Three. Swindon won this game 1-0, the clinching goal being scored in the closing minutes by Roger Smart.

Roger Smart, scorer of the goal that clinched promotion.

This cartoon from the club programme was to be of no avail in preventing large numbers of the crowd rushing on to the ground to celebrate.

The players who won promotion in the 1962/63 season. Back row, left to right: Mike Summerbee, Bobby Woodruff, John Trollope, Owen Dawson, Bill Atkins, Keith Morgan, Mike Turner, Ken McPherson, John Smith, Maurice Owen. Front row: Colin Huxford, Arnold Darcy, Ernie Hunt, Willie Harber, Harry Cousins (trainer), Keith Colsell, John Stevens, Roger Smart, Don Rogers, Cliff Jackson.

Swindon supporters who travelled to Bristol on Saturday

This picture from October 1962 shows how the dress and nature of football supporters have changed.

Wilf Castle (second left), who was chairman of Swindon for eighteen years before retiring and being created president, cuts the promotion celebration cake with Mayor Cockram. Also in the picture are Cliff Jackson, Mike Turner, Eric Lane, Cecil Green and Keith Morgan.

The original Swindon Town badge shared the motto 'Healthy and Industrious' with the town itself and was much loved by more traditionally-minded supporters who decried its replacement with logos – which were described by one fan as a traffic sign and a skid mark!

The board of directors who oversaw Swindon's first promotion season, 1962-1963. Back row, left to right: -?-, -?-, Reg Fricker, Ken Wilmer, -?-. Front row: ? Davies, Tom Hamilton, Wilf Castle, Eric Lane, Cecil Green.

Ernie Hunt scores Swindon's first ever goal in Division Two, watched by John Stevens (number 9). The match ended in a 3-0 victory over Scunthorpe. Town took maximum points from their first six fixtures to go top of the table, but failed to maintain their early momentum.

During the 1960s, Swindon Town had a team in the local 'Midnight' cricket league. It must have been excellent for morale that director Cecil Green, the coaching staff and the players all mucked in together. In this picture, from left to right, back row: Jack Conley, Rod Thomas, Owen Dawson, Keith Morgan, Cecil Green, Maurice Owen, Jimmy Giles. Front row: Keith Colsell, Jimmy Lawson, John Trollope, Don Rogers, Ken Skeen.

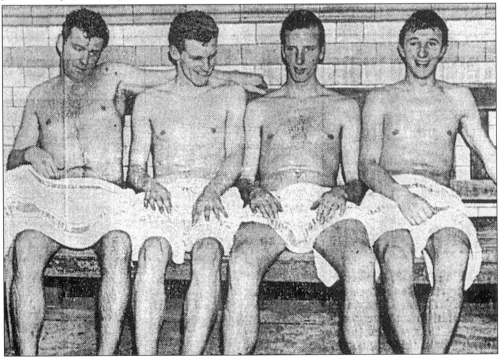

A turkish bath for John Stevens, John Trollope, Bill Atkins and Mike Summerbee.

The injury and illness of Ernie Hunt, their England Under-23 International, was crucial to Swindon's failure in 1964/65. Here, Harry Cousins and Jack Conley help him off after he had given Town the lead against Rotherham, only to suffer injury later in the match.

Desperate defence by Gordon Atherton and Ken Mcpherson in the last match of the 1964/65 season at the Dell Southampton. Town lost 2-1 and because Northampton (who needed a point for promotion) and Portsmouth (who needed a point to stay up) drew later that day, Town were relegated to Division Three.

BERT (A. S.) DAVIES, a local recruit, joined the Club in 1912/13, was then transferred to Middlesbrough, served in the Army in World War I, rejoined Swindon Town after the War ended, and joined Luton Town for a short spell in 1927. He returned as scout and after World War II became Assistant Manager under Mr. Louis Page. He is still active in Club affairs through the 63 Club. A most interesting article by Mr Davies will be found in last year's Handbook.

HARRY COUSINS joined the Club from Chesterfield in 1932, was appointed Assistant Trainer in 1937, First Team Trainer in 1950, and Youth Team Manager in 1969. He is still giving sterling service to the Club.

Courtesy Wiltshire Newspapers

MAURICE OWEN joined the Club in 1946 from Abingdon Town and scored a hat-trick in his first match against Watford. Centre-forward until 1957 and then to centre-half in 1959 and was Team Captain. Appointed Assistant Secretary in retirement, then became Coach and Reserve Team Trainer and was appointed First Team Trainer in 1969.

Courtesy Wiltshire Newspapers

Mr. RON MORSE
General Manager Swindon Town Football Co. Ltd.

Courtesy Wiltshire Newspapers

Four stalwart club servants who were prominent under Bert Head but were to go on serving the club after his departure.

Five

Danny's Double

Chairman Wilf Castle greets Danny Williams on his arrival as manager in 1965.

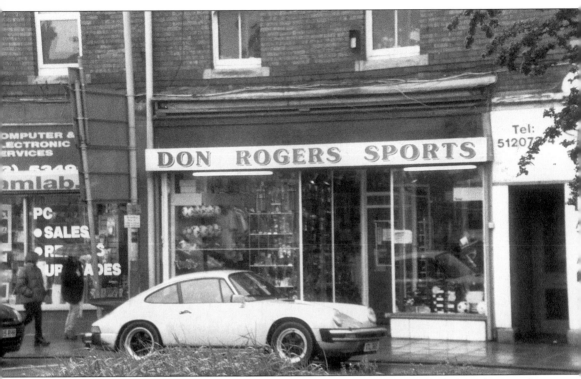

Swindon encouraged star winger Don Rogers to stay at the County Ground by helping him purchase a sports shop in Faringdon Road, which he still runs to this day.

This photograph of Don in his shop perhaps shows why Bob Wilson had more to fear than Jack Nicklaus.

Left: Peter Downsborough was a reliable goalkeeper, who gave what was probably his best display for Swindon in the League Cup final of 1969. *Right:* Welsh international Rod Thomas, who holds the record for most caps won while playing for Swindon Town.

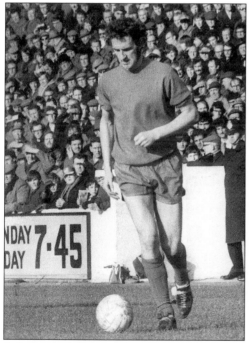 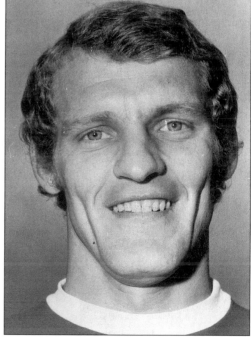

Left: Frank Burrows, one of three new signings made by Danny Williams at the start of the 1968/69 campaign. *Right:* John Trollope, whose club record of 368 consecutive appearances ended at Hartlepool where he suffered a broken arm in a goal-less draw on 24 August 1968.

Danny Williams and Jack Conley giving some advice to Rod Thomas before extra time in the League Cup semi-final decider with Burnley at the Hawthorns in 1969.

Jack Smith (arm aloft, centre) salutes the extra-time goal by Peter Noble (far left) which took Swindon to Wembley.

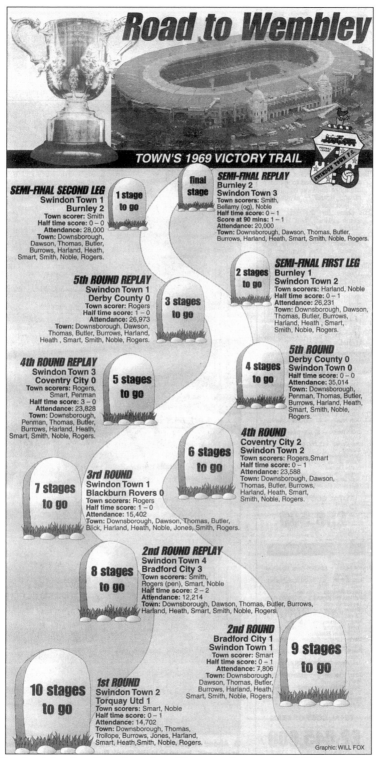

Road to Wembley

TOWN'S 1969 VICTORY TRAIL

SEMI-FINAL SECOND LEG
Swindon Town 1
Burnley 2
Town scorer: Smith
Half time score: 0 – 0
Attendance: 28,000
Town: Downsborough, Dawson, Thomas, Butler, Burrows, Harland, Heath, Smart, Smith, Noble, Rogers.

1 stage to go

final stage

SEMI-FINAL REPLAY
Burnley 2
Swindon Town 3
Town scorers: Smith, Bellamy (og), Noble.
Half time score: 0 – 1
Score at 90 mins: 1 – 1
Attendance: 20,000
Town: Downsborough, Dawson, Thomas, Butler, Burrows, Harland, Heath, Smart, Smith, Noble, Rogers.

5th ROUND REPLAY
Swindon Town 1
Derby County 0
Town scorer: Rogers
Half time score: 1 – 0
Attendance: 26,973
Town: Downsborough, Dawson, Thomas, Butler, Burrows, Harland, Heath , Smart, Smith, Noble, Rogers.

3 stages to go

2 stages to go

SEMI-FINAL FIRST LEG
Burnley 1
Swindon Town 2
Town scorers: Harland, Noble
Half time score: 0 – 1
Attendance: 26,231
Town: Downsborough, Dawson, Thomas, Butler, Burrows, Harland, Heath , Smart, Smith, Noble, Rogers.

4th ROUND REPLAY
Swindon Town 3
Coventry City 0
Town scorers: Rogers, Smart, Penman
Half time score: 3 – 0
Attendance: 23,828
Town: Downsborough, Penman, Thomas, Butler, Burrows, Harland, Heath, Smart, Smith, Noble, Rogers.

5 stages to go

4 stages to go

5th ROUND
Derby County 0
Swindon Town 0
Half time score: 0 – 0
Attendance: 35,014
Town: Downsborough, Penman, Thomas, Butler, Burrows, Harland, Heath, Smart, Smith, Noble, Rogers.

4th ROUND
Coventry City 2
Swindon Town 2
Town scorers: Rogers, Smart
Half time score: 0 – 1
Attendance: 23,588
Town: Downsborough, Dawson, Thomas, Butler, Burrows, Harland, Heath, Smart, Smith, Noble, Rogers.

6 stages to go

3rd ROUND
Swindon Town 1
Blackburn Rovers 0
Town scorers: Rogers
Half time score: 1 – 0
Attendance: 15,402
Town: Downsborough, Dawson, Thomas, Butler, Blick, Harland, Heath, Noble, Jones, Smith, Rogers.

7 stages to go

2nd ROUND REPLAY
Swindon Town 4
Bradford City 3
Town scorers: Smith, Rogers (pen), Smart, Noble
Half time score: 2 – 2
Attendance: 12,214
Town: Downsborough, Dawson, Thomas, Butler, Burrows, Harland, Heath, Smart, Smith, Noble, Rogers.

8 stages to go

2nd ROUND
Bradford City 1
Swindon Town 1
Town scorer: Smart
Half time score: 0 – 1
Attendance: 7,806
Town: Downsborough, Dawson, Thomas, Butler, Burrows, Harland, Heath, Smart, Smith, Noble, Rogers.

9 stages to go

10 stages to go

1st ROUND
Swindon Town 2
Torquay Utd 1
Town scorers: Smart, Noble
Half time score: 0 – 1
Attendance: 14,702
Town: Downsborough, Thomas, Trollope, Burrows, Jones, Harland, Smart, Heath, Smith, Noble, Rogers.

Graphic: WILL FOX

This *Evening Advertiser* chart shows how Town made it to the 1969 League Cup final.

Danny and his men as portrayed in an *Evening Advertiser* cartoon.

Don Rogers celebrates the first of his two extra-time goals that gave Swindon victory over Arsenal in the League Cup final.

Rogers' second goal, which came after he had dribbled from the halfway line.

Downsborough dives fearlessly to save at the feet of Arsenal's Bobby Gould. This was one of many fine stops he made during the final.

Post-final celebrations for, from left to right: Roger Smart (scorer of the first goal), Joe Butler, John Trollope, Peter Noble, Don Rogers, Stan Harland, Rod Thomas (behind) and Don Heath (partially obscured).

A reunion of the team that won the League Cup. The cardboard cut-out behind these players was made for a TV company, which made a programme about the reunion. It ended its days as a makeshift wall for players practising free kicks on the training ground.

The players are joined by physiotherapist Kevin Morris.

Bob Jefferies took over as the club secretary from Ron Morse and continued to give loyal service until his own retirement in the 1980s. Here he is seen wearing the tie that Swindon brought out to commemorate the Wembley appearance.

The Swindon Town Robinettes, seen posing here on Stratton Bank, brightened the scene at many Swindon matches in the late 1960s and early '70s.

An eighty-ninth minute goal at Rotherham, seen here on its way into the net, gave Swindon a point in a 1-1 draw which guaranteed promotion

Chris Jones was the scorer of the goal that ensured promotion.

Six

Foreign Triumph
Domestic Failures

Despite winning the League Cup in 1969, Swindon were not allowed to enter the Inter Cities
Fairs Cup. By way of compensation, a two-leg match was played with AS Roma. Swindon won
this handsome trophy by an aggregate of 5-2.

The Anglo Italian Cup won in 1970. It was a particular triumph as it was played on the ground of the opponents, Napoli.

Fred Ford's first season in charge (1969/70) saw Swindon overcome teams from the top divisions of both the Italian League and Football League to win the Anglo Italian Cup. In this photograph, the Napoli and Swindon teams line up before the final.

Peter Noble heads the first of Swindon's three goals against Napoli.

The defeat of the home team by 3-0 did not please the Italian fans, who are shown hurling broken seating onto the pitch.

Stan Harland holds the Anglo Italian Trophy aloft. The tall figure, third from left, was Mick Kearns of Oxford United, who acted as understudy to Town goalkeeper Roy Jones.

The squad for the 1970/71 season pose with the Anglo Italian League Cup Winners Cup and Anglo Italian Cup. It includes most of the squad who the previous season took Town to the FA Cup sixth round for the first time since 1924 and, by finishing fifth in Division Two, reached the highest League position the club had achieved to that date.

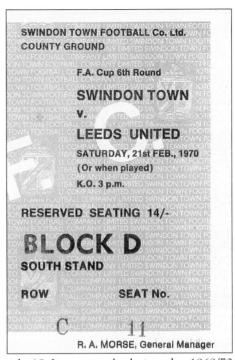

SWINDON TOWN FOOTBALL Co. Ltd.
COUNTY GROUND

F.A. Cup 6th Round

SWINDON TOWN
v.
LEEDS UNITED

SATURDAY, 21st FEB., 1970
(Or when played)
K.O. 3 p.m.

RESERVED SEATING 14/-

BLOCK D

SOUTH STAND

ROW   SEAT No.

C   11

R. A. MORSE, General Manager

Arthur Horsfield was the club's leading scorer with 18 League goals during the 1969/70 campaign. Swindon reached the last eight of the FA Cup in 1970 for the first time since 1924. This is a ticket stub for that match.

Stan Harland leads out the Swindon Town team for the FA Cup sixth round tie with Leeds United in 1971, which Town lost 2-0.

John Trollope smashes home the only goal in a 1-0 home win over Watford on 28 March 1970, as Town push for promotion to Division One.

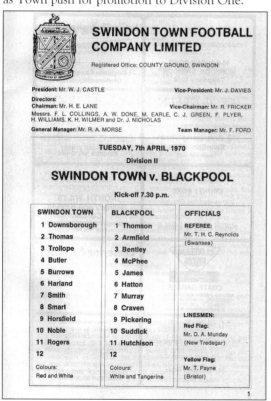

SWINDON TOWN FOOTBALL COMPANY LIMITED

Registered Office: COUNTY GROUND, SWINDON

President: Mr. W. J. CASTLE   **Vice-President:** Mr. J. DAVIES

Directors:
Chairman: Mr. H. E. LANE   **Vice-Chairman:** Mr. R. FRICKER
Messrs. F. L. COLLINGS, A. W. DONE, M. EARLE, C. J. GREEN, F. PLYER, H. WILLIAMS, K. H. WILMER and Dr. J. NICHOLAS
General Manager: Mr. R. A. MORSE   **Team Manager:** Mr. F. FORD

TUESDAY, 7th APRIL, 1970

Division II

SWINDON TOWN v. BLACKPOOL

Kick-off 7.30 p.m.

SWINDON TOWN	BLACKPOOL	OFFICIALS
1 Downsborough	1 Thomson	**REFEREE:**
2 Thomas	2 Armfield	Mr. T. H. C. Reynolds
3 Trollope	3 Bentley	(Swansea)
4 Butler	4 McPhee	
5 Burrows	5 James	
6 Harland	6 Hatton	
7 Smith	7 Murray	
8 Smart	8 Craven	
9 Horsfield	9 Pickering	**LINESMEN:**
10 Noble	10 Suddick	**Red Flag:**
11 Rogers	11 Hutchison	Mr. D. A. Munday
12	12	(New Tredegar)
Colours:	Colours:	**Yellow Flag:**
Red and White	White and Tangerine	Mr. T. Payne
		(Bristol)

1

The front of the programme for the match with Blackpool in 1970.

Arthur Horsfield giving Swindon a fourth minute lead against Blackpool. However, the Seasiders equalised and thus virtually ended Town's hopes of promotion.

Dave Mackay, who was installed as a player at the start of the 1971/72 season and replaced Fred Ford as manager in November.

Signed from Liverpool during the 1970/71 season, Steve Peplow never fulfilled his early promise.

The black shorts and socks worn in this picture were seen by many fans as a bad omen. The players in the picture are, from left to right, back row: John Trollope, Peter Downsborough, Roger Smart. Middle row: Ron Potter, Terry Hubbard, Rod Thomas, Frank Burrows, Des Anderson (assistant manager). Front row: Don Rogers, Steve Peplow, Ron Howells, Dave Mackay, Ray Treacy, Joe Butler.

The South Stand was opened in August 1971 and for some years dwarfed the rest of the County Ground. Originally, it increased the seating capacity of the ground to 8,300. This picture was taken in 1974, when it was decided to demolish the old North Stand seating which had thus far been retained.

A view inside the dressing room, under the new stand.

This aerial view of the County Ground must have been taken between the construction of the New South Stand and the demolition of the three buildings in the right foreground. These had housed the Supporters Club, among other things, which was later relocated in the new stand.

Bob Wilson advances from the Arsenal goal to foil Don Rogers in the FA Cup third round match in 1972, watched by 32,000 spectators – the biggest crowd ever at the County Ground.

A board meeting during the 1970s. From left to right: L. Smart, W. Dore, C. Day, C. Cowley (vice-chairman), R. Morse (finance manager), C. Green (chairman), R. Jefferies (secretary), R. Stephenson, R. Kearsey and G. Whittock.

Joe Butler was player of the year in both 1969/70 and 1972/73. During his career with Swindon he played in every position except goalkeeper. Here, he can be seen holding his Player of the Year trophy with Ron Morse and Bob Jefferies.

Joe with wife, Ann, daughter, Joanna, and son, Joe.

'One or other – not both' was the party line when Don Rogers left to join Crystal Palace in 1972, but the following November saw Rod Thomas move to join former Town manager Dave Mackay at Derby.

The high dropout rate of apprentice footballers is illustrated by this picture of Youth Manager Les Allen with his team. Although they reached the Youth Cup fifth round, only David Syrett (seated second left) became a regular first team player at the County Ground.

At one time, there were hopes that Chris Porter, a fast winger who was willing to take on defenders, might make the grade but his 36 League performances were spread over four seasons and produced just 4 goals.

Danny Williams, who returned to the County Ground for a second spell as manager in March 1974.

Trevor Anderson was signed from Manchester United. He scored 35 League goals for Town before joining Peterborough in 1977.

West Ham goalkeeper Mervyn Day foils Trevor Anderson in an FA Cup fourth round replay during January 1975. Anderson scored Swindon's only goal in a 2-1 defeat.

Frank Burrows, who was taken on in a coaching role in 1976, helps Chris Kamara with his heading.

Steve Aizelwood was noted for his strength in the air, which is demonstrated here in a match with Gillingham in 1977 which ended in a 3-2 win for Town. Colin Prophett is the other Town player in the picture.

Steve Aizelwood was signed from Newport County in 1976. By the time he departed to Portsmouth (for three times what he cost) he had made over 100 appearances for Swindon.

A £22,000 fee brought Roy Carter to the County Ground from Hereford United in December 1977. He was to make well over 200 appearances for Town before moving on to Torquay United.

Cecil Green is perhaps the only man to be player, scout, chairman and president of a Football League club.

Seven

Into the Eighties

Bobby Smith took over as Swindon manager in May 1978.

Wilf Trantor came to Swindon as Bob Smith's assistant. His pre-match warm ups were an interesting innovation. It was after his departure for personal reasons at the start of the 1980/81 season that things began to go wrong for Town.

This picture of Brian Williams in action against Wimbledon shows how fencing had been erected to enclose away supporters, while falling gates meant only two blocks of the old South Stand were open.

Brian Williams, whose ferocious tackling earned him the affectionate nickname 'Animal' from Town supporters, seen in action against Brian Talbot at Highbury, where a 1-1 draw set the stage for a dramatic replay at the County Ground.

Safety regulations and all-seater stadia meant the end of scenes like this one on 26 January 1980 when 25,673 crowded into the County Ground to see Town draw 0-0 with Tottenham in the FA Cup fourth round.

Football disasters of the early 1980s were to mean more stringent safety regulations – including checks on the strengths of crush barriers like those being carried out here on Stratton Bank.

Ian Miller, who followed manager Bobby Smith from Bury to Swindon and played a vital part in Swindon's run to the League Cup semi-final in 1980.

Swindon marked their centenary with a match in 1981 against FA Cup holders Ipswich Town. Jimmy Allan foils Eric Gates as Charlie Henry and Kevin Baddeley, both products of the Swindon Boys team, look on.

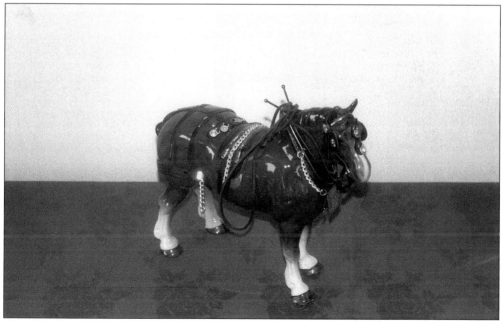

This Shire horse was presented to the club by Ipswich to mark their visit and can be seen in the Trophy cabinet to this day.

Two pictures from Swindon's last home match of the 1981/82 season. *Above*: Roy Carter wins an aerial challenge watched by Paul Rideout. *Below*: Mark Kendall in the Newport goal is watched by Russell Lewis as he produces a save to a shot by David Peach, which limited Town to a 1-1 draw. Away defeats at Portsmouth and Newport followed and consigned Swindon to the basement of the Football League.

Although the 1981/82 season ended with the disappointment of Town being relegated to Division Four for the first time in their history, a win over Oxford near the end of the season gave hopes of survival. In this picture, Roy Carter celebrates scoring Town's second goal in a 3-2 win.

Paul Batty and Kevin Baddeley were typical examples of the youth team products with which John Trollope had to try to rebuild Swindon's fortunes, after taking over as manager in November 1980.

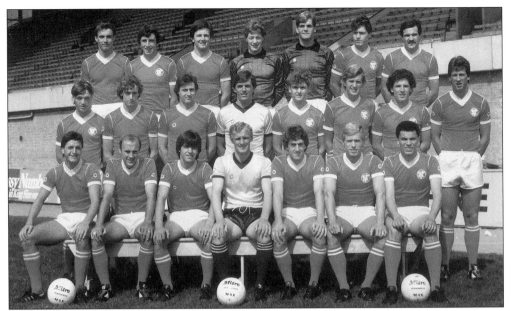

The Swindon squad for the 1982/83 season. From left to right, back row: Jimmy Quinn, Russell Lewis, Charlie Henry, Jimmy Allan, Mark Stevens, Paul Rideout, Andy Rowland. Middle row: Martin Blackler, Brian Hughes, Howard Pritchard, Ken Beamish (assistant manager), David Bristow, Roy Carter, Kevin Baddeley, David Round. Front row: Mick Graham, Gary Emmanuel, Paul Batty, John Trollope (manager), Ray Baverstock, Leigh Barnard, Gary Williams.

Despite a disappointing season in the League, Swindon made respectable progress in the FA Cup during the 1982/83 season, reaching the fourth round. Here, Paul Rideout is beaten in the air during the second round replay at Brentford, which ended in a 3-1 victory for Town after extra time.

Left: Ken Beamish, who had been appointed by John Trollope as his assistant, was promoted to the manager's chair in April 1983, only to find himself surplus to requirements when new sponsors Lowndes Lambert demanded the appointment of a big name player-manager at the start of the 1984/85 season. *Right:* Paul Richardson was Ken Beamish's assistant. He made 7 League appearances early in the 1983/84 season.

Jimmy Allan made the last of his 371 League appearances for Town against Rochdale in October 1983 when a broken arm brought an untimely end to his career. He earned a small place in the history books of soccer when, on 30 January 1974, he became the first professional to decline to play on a Sundays

Jimmy Quinn scoring one of his two goals during a 7-0 FA Cup first round victory for Swindon at Kettering.

Alan Mayes, seen here shooting for goal in a match against Rochdale, was Town's leading scorer during the 1983/84 season. In all, he scored 65 goals during two spells with Town.

Eight

Lou Macari's Red and White Army

New sponsors Lowndes Lambert insisted on a big name player-manager and Lou Macari proved to be a wonderful choice.

Lou Macari's first season in charge at Swindon (1984/85) was hardly a bed of roses. It included a humiliating home defeat by Dagenham in the FA Cup. Here, Peter Coyne and Alan Mayes, who scored Town's only goal in the 2-1 defeat, watch an acrobatic save by the Dagenham 'keeper.

Harry Gregg had encouraged Lou to apply for the manager's job at Swindon and became his assistant, but disagreements led to his departure at Easter in 1985.

Andy Rowlands (left), who was soon to join the coaching staff, and Scott Endersby. Both players were ever present during Lou's first season in charge and are displaying the logo of the new club sponsors.

Charlie Henry shoots for goal in the 1985 Littlewoods Cup match against Torquay at the County Ground in 1985.

It was a Littlewoods Cup victory over Sunderland which sparked the successful 1985/86 season into life. Here, Peter Coyne slots home the goal which took the tie into extra time and paved the way for Swindon's victory.

Steve White celebrates scoring one of the many goals of his career with Swindon. This particular strike was an equaliser to give Town a point in a 1-1 draw with Chester and, like many of his goals, was scored after he came on as a substitute.

A 3-1 win over Burnley saw Swindon shatter a sixty-two year old club record by winning fourteen consecutive home games. In this picture, Charlie Henry (arm aloft) salutes scoring the first goal.

Promotion to Division Three was clinched with a 4-2 victory over Chester. In this picture Bryan Wade, number 10, heads home Town's third goal.

Left: Charlie Henry began his career as a defender but was transformed by Lou Macari into a rampaging midfielder, who was to finish the 1985/86 season as leading goalscorer. *Right*: Bryan Wade had been working as a stonemason before joining Swindon, where his goalscoring efforts helped Swindon to a record 102 points in the 1985/86 season.

Manager of the Month awards created something of a problem for Lou, who was a teetotaller. He usually solved it by giving the supporters a tot or handing the bottles over to a charity. In the background of this photograph can be seen the old stand, which was closed due to new safety regulations following the Bradford fire disaster.

Sometimes it was only weather that could halt the progress of Lou's Red and White Army. The Darlington manager and referee discuss the snowbound pitch in company with Town Chairman Brian Hillier and Lou Macari during the 1985/86 season.

Colin Gordon, who scored many valuable goals during the Championship triumph of 1985/86.

The squad that won Division Four. From left to right, back row: John Trollope (assistant manager), Leigh Barnard, Chris Kamara, Dave Bamber, Colin Gordon, Dave Cole, Kenny Allen, Charlie Henry, Colin Calderwood, Dave Hockaday, Andy Rowland, Chris Ramsey, Kevin Morris (physiotherapist). Front row: Brian Wade, Peter Coyne, Paul Roberts, Lou Macari (manager), Derek Hall, Tony Evans, David Moss.

Left: The Canon Trophy for the Division Four Championship, which Swindon won with an all time record of 102 points. *Right*: Chris Ramsey, who signed from Brighton, proved a dependable right-back.

Kenny Allan salutes the crowd after collecting an award at the end of the 1985/86 season.

Fraser Digby, signed originally on loan from Manchester United, was to go on to give ten years of service to Swindon and beat Sam Burton's record number of appearances by a Swindon goalkeeper.

A large crowd packed into the County Ground for the Easter 1987 fixture, with promotion rivals Bournemouth. In this picture, Jimmy Quinn is unable to make contact, while Steve White, Chris Kamara, Tim Parkin and Leigh Barnard look on.

An unusual role for Jimmy Quinn, seen here as stand-in 'keeper in a Freight Rover Trophy match against Aldershot after Digby had been sent off.

Dave Bamber was the scorer of the first goal in the semi-final promotion play off in 1987. Swindon were trailing 2-0 at the time but recovered to beat Wigan 3-2.

Peter Coyne, Fraser Digby (Player of the Year) and Charlie Henry after a 2-1 victory at the County Ground over Gillingham, which took the play-off final to a third match.

Steve White scores the first of his two goals which won the play-off final with Gillingham and ensured Swindon a place in Division Two.

Left: Bryan Wade carries two goal hero Steve from the field. *Right:* Dave Hockaday, minus strip, after the victory over Gillingham in the play-off final at Selhurst Park. Lou Macari had ordered his players back out to share their champagne with supporters.

Nine
Ossie and Glenn

Celebrations after the 1-0 victory over Sunderland. From left to right, back row: Andy Rowlands, Duncan Shearer, Fitzroy Simpson, Jon Gittens, Paul Bodin, Dave Hockaday, Steve White, Chic Bates, Frazer Digby, Ross Maclaren, Ossie Ardiles. Front row: Alan McLoughlin, Tom Jones, Colin Calderwood, Dave Kerslake, Steve Foley.

Left: Originally a player at the County Ground, Chic Bates returned to serve as assistant manager under both Lou Macari and Ossie Ardiles. *Right*: Ossie Ardiles, who took over the manager's role from Lou Macari, in a relaxed family pose with his wife, Silvia, and younger son, Frederico.

Alan McLoughlin, who scored the goal that gave Town their 1-0 win over Sunderland in the play-off final.

Ossie and Chic continue celebrations with their players on the coach. Celebrations were cut short a few days later when the Football League relegated Town by two divisions because of illegal payments.

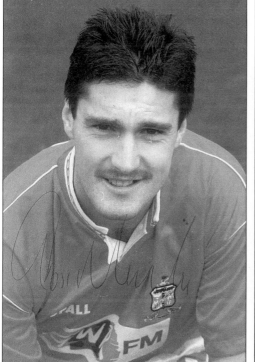 

Left: Ross Maclaren, who was to enjoy two Wembley triumphs with Town before joining the coaching staff. *Right:* Colin Calderwood, captain of Swindon during their remarkable rise from Division Four to the Premiership.

Left: Dave King, the Swindon Town secretary who received a six month suspended sentence after pleading guilty to conspiracy to defraud the Inland Revenue. *Right*: Gary Herbert, who took over as chairman from Brian Hillier, was jailed for his part in making illegal payments to players.

Red and white balloons go up before the play off final against Leicester City in May 1993. Swindon were bravely fighting to regain the Premiership status denied them by the footballing authorities two years earlier.

Martin Ling rushes to congratulate Glenn Hoddle, who has just scored Town's opening goal in the play-off final.

Craig Maskell fires home Swindon's second goal in the match with Leicester City.

Craig Maskell celebrates as Shaun Taylor, prostrate on ground, heads the third Town goal.

Having squandered a three goal lead, a late penalty by Paul Bodin finally gave Swindon a place in the Premiership and sparked these celebrations.

Paul Bodin, whose penalty at Wembley was not the first vital goal he scored for Swindon during the 1992/93 season.

Paul Bodin who with less than ten minutes to go had to step forward and score one of the most important penalty kicks of his career. With Leicester City having come back from being three down to level the scores at 3-3, the foul on Steve White left Town's Premier League ambitions in the hands of our Welsh International who gave Leicester keeper Kevin Poole no chance with the resultant spot-kick.

Shaun Taylor was a pillar of strength in defence and also contributed some valuable headed goals.

Glenn Hoddle and John Gorman, the partnership that finally brought Premiership football to Swindon.

The front cover of the programme for Swindon's first ever home match in the Premiership shows Paul Bodin, Craig Maskell, Glenn Hoddle and Shaun Taylor celebrating their Wembley success.

Ten

Recent Times

Left: Jan Aga Fjortoft, whose goalscoring and sense of fun endeared him to Swindon fans, is seen here in Napoleonic mood with Mayor David Glaholm. *Right:* Keith Scott, whose goal against Queens Park Rangers gave Swindon their first Premiership victory.

Had this Fjortoft goal not been disallowed it would have given Swindon a 2-0 lead at Maine Road and might have provided the launching pad for an escape from relegation, but the match ended in a 2-1 win for fellow strugglers Manchester City.

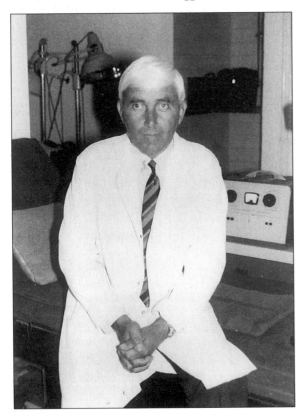

Kevin Morris had been a popular physiotherapist at the County Ground for many years when he committed suicide in 1994.

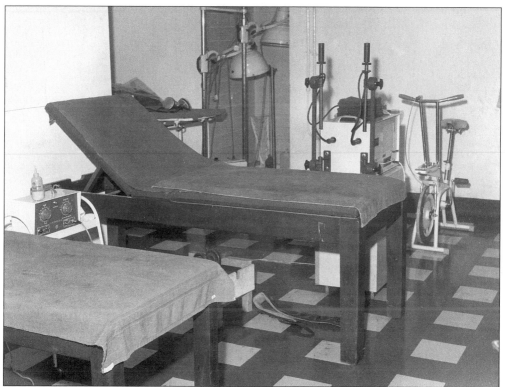

The excellent equipment in the treatment room had been built up over many years and was very much Kevin's Kingdom.

Director Cliff Puffett in front of the Intel Stand, which provided an additional 5,000 seats for the 1994/95 season.

Even the temper of the amiable John Gorman began to fray as poor results saw relegation followed by a slide to the middle of the Division One table. The axe finally fell following a defeat at Bristol City. Andy Rowland (looking at watch in the background) enjoyed a brief spell as caretaker manager before the appointment of Steve McMahon.

The celebrations of Joey Beauchamp (far left), Peter Thorne (number 10), Wayne Sullivan (number 2, hugging scorer Fjortoft) were short lived. This goal at Burnden Park put Town 3-1 up on aggregate, but Bolton scored three times in the last half hour to deny Swindon a place in the Coca Cola Cup final of 1995.

The sale of Fjortoft, as Town headed for a second relegation in consecutive seasons, brought an angry demonstration from fans after a 1-0 home defeat by Charlton in March 1995.

An all-too-common sight as Swindon slipped towards relegation was player-manager Steve McMahon involved in heated debate with referees. Sent off on his Town debut, later in the same season he suffered the same fate in the home League match against Bolton.

The men who sought to restore Swindon's fortunes in the 1995/96 season. From left to right: Andy Rowlands, Steve McMahon, Sir Seaton Wills, Cliff Puffett, Mike Spearman, Rikki Hunt, Peter Archer, Peter Godwin, Steven Hunt.

Scott Leitch and Peter Thorne celebrate the goal in a 1-1 draw at Blackpool that ensured Swindon returned to Divison One at the first time of asking.

Vince McCormack, Emma McCormack, Michael Bowden, Barbara McCormack, Debbie Bowden and Linda Bowden are the fans in happy mood after a 1-1 draw at Blackpool assured Swindon of promotion back to Division One in 1996.

The Mizuno Trophy was won by Swindon Town for having the best away results in the League during the 1995/96 season.

Outside the Town Hall, fans gather to salute Swindon Town becoming the Division Two champions of 1996.

Steve McMahon holds aloft the Division Two Trophy.

Steve McMahon with his Manager of the Month and the Second Division Manager of the Season awards.

Financial pressure forced the sale of Wayne Allison and marked a turning point in the club's fortunes. Manager McMahon resigned, but with gates falling the financial pressure became worse and the 1999/2000 season saw Town again fighting against relegation.

Gareth Hall shoots home Swindon's equaliser against fellow strugglers West Bromwich Albion in January 2000.

Scott Leitch, Town's captain during the 1999/2000 campaign, in action during the goal-less draw at Blackburn.

A sadly familiar sight during the 1999/2000 campaign, which was to end in relegation, was that of Swindon defenders arguing after a goal had been conceded – as has happened here in a match with Birmingham.

Alan Reeves heads a Barnsley effort off the line with Lee Collins covering behind, during Jimmy Quinn's last match in charge.

It was at times too much for Jimmy to watch as Town went down 2-1.

Frank Talia, left, collects the *Evening Advertiser* Player of the Season award prior to the Barnsley match.

Jamie Williams, right, who is the youngest player ever to appear in the League for Swindon, collects the Clive King Memorial Trophy for the Young Player of the Season for 1999/2000.

Looking to the future are chairman Cliff Puffett and Tom Brady, who worked together to get Swindon out of administration.

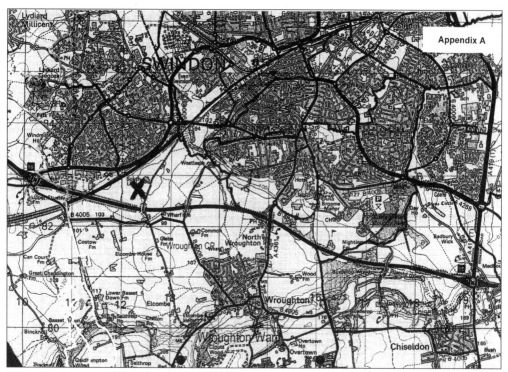

Appendix A

'X' marks the spot of the site which could be the new home of Swindon Town.